QUÉBEC

COOMBE BOOKS

CLB 2628
This 1991 edition published by Bramley Books.
© 1991 Colour Library Books Ltd., Godalming, Surrey, England.
© 1991 Illustrations: Miller Comstock, Inc., Toronto, Ontario, Canada
   and Colour Library Books Ltd., Godalming, Surrey, England.
Printed by Leefung-Asco Printers Ltd., Hong Kong.
All rights reserved.
ISBN 0 86283 865 7

I believe that Quebec is the most unique and exciting place in the world, but don't just take my word for it – ask any Québécois or Québécoise. We'd be pleased to tell you how we play, work and laugh harder than any other people due to our genuine sense of joy in what Quebec has become.

In a land that is more than twice the size of Texas, and three times the area of France, we have managed to carve for ourselves a magnificent place on the razor's edge of the modern world, while still preserving that rich European-style culture which remains such an important part of our everyday lives. That's not bad for just six-and-a-half million people. We're proud of what we have, and we love to share that experience with the visitors who are now coming in ever greater numbers to enjoy all the pleasures of "la belle province". There's always something happening in Quebec – usually something new and different, but always something Québécois.

In many ways the people of Quebec still reflect their early seventeenth-century beginnings. Quebec is where it all began in the northern part of North America. A few early explorers, looking for a shorter route to the East, sailed up the St. Lawrence River and laid claim to most of this unknown continent in the name of France. In fact Jacques Cartier, the first one to arrive in the Montreal region in 1535, was so convinced he'd reached the Orient that he named the area China, and, as one of those ironies of history, it's still "Lachine" today. Even worse for poor Cartier, he returned to France loaded down with worthless iron pyrites, presenting them to the king as "diamonds from the New World".

The king was not amused, and the development of Quebec had to wait for almost a century.

By 1608, however, the kings of France were beginning to send out settlers to "la Nouvelle France", New France. In the final analysis, they sent a total of only 8,000 people during the 150-year period that the colony remained under French control. By comparison, Québécois number 6,000,000 today, not counting 5,000,000 or so descendants who have migrated to various parts of the United States, which is quite an extraordinary growth!

It didn't take long for the settlers to realize that they weren't living in Europe any more. Indeed, the transition must have been quite shocking in those early years and from the very outset, the conditions began to mould a new breed of person. These people changed indelibly as they adapted to their new home: their lifestyle, their language and their customs all began to take on a distinctly North American flavour. They were becoming French Canadian even then.

Fortunately for these newcomers, they were able to borrow a great deal from the natives, who taught them how to thrive in the North American wilderness. They came to love it. City-bred soldiers and laborers soon evolved into a rugged, independent people who kept what they could from their European heritage, while accepting the realities of their new land. In many ways we're still doing this today.

Yet we probably wouldn't be here at all if it hadn't been for that most vital of lifelines to the outside world, the St. Lawrence River. The explorers, the settlers and the fur traders all owed their ultimate success to the St. Lawrence and its intricate system of tributaries. From the earliest days it was their surest source of food, and the only dependable roadway. In fact, most land divisions in farming communities still reflect the early stipulation that all farms be allotted river frontage. You can see it plainly from the air as the long, thin strips of land seem to defy the compass in order to line up with the water's edge. Even today anyone arriving by boat can get that same sense of community which existed then, that "one big village of farmhouses" which lined both sides of the river for several hundred miles, and which had become a hallmark of the colony as early as the mid-1700s.

The river itself stretches into the very heartland of Quebec, well over 1,000 miles from the sea. Indeed, just east of Quebec City, a full 750 miles from the Atlantic, the river is still saline and swells daily with twenty-foot tides! They say that a drop of water from the St. Lawrence system runs through the veins of every Québécois. Maybe it's true. We still need to be near water today. If we're away from it for too long, we begin to get uncomfortable, and have to seek it out.

Most of all, though, being Québécois means enjoying the four seasons to the full. This has become a vital part of our lifestyle and part of our "joie de vivre". Over the years we have found the formula to live each season as it comes, and as Québécois we need to savour them. We say in Quebec that there is no such thing as poor weather, only the wrong clothes.

I happen to be one of those who enjoy winter most of all. My fondest childhood memories are centred on snow. I recall building snow forts in anticipation of a snowball war, and skating on an outdoor rink on a chilly evening with the ice crackling as I held onto the waist of a special girl and tried to skate in time to

the music, careful to avoid the embarrassment of falling down or − even worse − crashing into somebody else. Winter also meant getting out after the latest snowfall, determined to roll the biggest snowman on the block, and not realizing until I was much older that my mother always made sure to save an old hat and a scarf to dress him. We had to keep him warm.

Winter brings out the best in the Québécois. We don't hibernate − we use it. Every respectable household has a set of cross-country skis for each member of the family. In fact there are many who are convinced that weekends were specifically devised for friends and relatives to get together and travel some of the thousands of miles of spectacular ski trails that have been prepared for them throughout the province. To do this is pure exhilaration. At least once a season you may have an experience you wish to relive for weeks, such as skiing around a tight bend on a crisp, sunny day − there's new snow on the trees, everything is silent − and then suddenly right there in front of you is a deer, or a porcupine, or a family of raccoons. It's inspirational − certainly something to share later over a cognac.

For many Québécois winter also means downhill skiing. On holidays and weekends roads begin to congest early in the morning as thousands of city-folk make their way to the province's many picturesque slopes. Others bring skidoos, cutting their own trails through forests and fields that usually only receive summer visitors.

Yet without a doubt ice hockey remains the most popular winter sport in Quebec. It is the great leveller in Quebec society. Whether you're playing or watching, you come to the game without any symbols of class, any pretentions, any politics. You come because you love it. Québécois children are first put on skates at five or six years old and are taught to hold onto a chair as they push it around the ice until they can finally skate on their own. It's like learning how to walk all over again, but it's wonderful once you've learned, and you never forget it. It stays with you for life.

And when you aren't playing hockey, you can watch this, one of the most amazing spectator sports ever devised. Several matches a week are shown live on television, but you really have to go to the Montreal Forum or the Québec Colisée to understand what hockey is all about – the speed, the intensity, the "oos" and "aahs" after a good pass or a solid check, and the fierce rivalry which exists between teams, especially when the Montréal Canadiens play the Québec Nordiques. Those tickets are sold out the day they go on sale and are worth a king's ransom. All this for the opportunity to see great hockey, to cheer for your team, "boo" the opposition, and scream at the referees – just for being referees. Everyone goes home hoarse, but smiling – regardless of the final outcome. It's addictive. More than once I've made a transatlantic telephone call to learn who won a crucial game!

Winter also affects what happens in the home. As the days get colder and shorter, we lay in a reasonable supply of liquid body warmers in anticipation of those long winter evenings spent with old friends, eating good food and sipping fine wine. There is always a great deal of soul-lifting talk, but at least as much time spent laughing too. There's something comforting about spending an evening with friends as the wind howls outside and the snow blows onto the windows like needles. There's an atmosphere of understanding and togetherness that is difficult to explain.

And just as winter begins to feel just a little too long, after twelve or fourteen feet of snow has fallen, we finally get that first really warm day hinting that spring is just around the corner. The internal clocks of all living things are triggered, ready for the explosion of nature which lies ahead. Now a billion buds are impatient to become summer leaves, tulips are pushing through the last layer of winter snow, and birds are preparing their nests, as Canada geese return to their northern breeding grounds, impressive in their spectacular "V" formations as they fly overhead.

It is wonderful to feel those first warm rays of sun on cheeks that have become chapped by winter winds. The sun comes as a tonic, and heralds a time of refreshing renewal. For the Québécois it is also a kind of liberation. We can shed a few layers of our winter clothing, packing them away in the cedar closet until the cycle comes full circle. Boots are always the last to go. They have to be kept for the other side of spring – the last marathon shovelling session, the water run-off, the slush in the streets as the ice melts. But it's a small price to pay for the coming heat.

The entire province changes gear with the arrival of spring. For thousands of farmers in Quebec, spring means preparing their machinery for summer planting. The St. Lawrence Seaway is once again open for ships, and students, though distracted by the activities of the season, begin to study for final exams in anticipation of the long-awaited summer holidays. For all of us, spring means maple syrup. This is the season when we can meet at the sugar shacks to be found throughout the province. We have "sugaring-off parties", great social events, and in the process we get our annual "transfusion" of God's most precious nectar.

For some, spring means the beginning of the baseball season, that wonderfully civilized sport that goes on until October. We love baseball in Quebec. It is revealing that the Montreal Expos have among the highest attendance records in the league, in spite of the fact that almost all the games are carried live on both radio and television.

That's the odd thing about baseball. In many ways, it captures the very essence of Quebec.

It's an American sport, of course, but one that's been adopted so wholeheartedly by the Québécois that you might well think that it had been invented by us. And in a very unexpected way, we did make a lasting contribution to the sport. In a conscious effort to strengthen Quebec's cultural identity, the appropriate government-sponsored bodies devised an entire technical French vocabulary for baseball. Not surprisingly, the Québécois have learned the lexicon and pride themselves on using the French-language terms correctly. Adaptation at its best means integration, rather than assimilation. That's the Quebec of today.

Maybe baseball is so popular in Quebec because it gives us the chance to sit outside in the summer sun. In fact, to be entirely honest, the Québécois are somewhat obsessed with the sun. We love our winters, to be sure, but we are also the world's champion sun-seekers. At the first hint of summer off come the clothes as we lie prostrate and unmoving, the maximum amount of skin exposed to any sunshine which may choose to bless us from above. And when we can't get enough sun at home, there's a steady stream of Québécois on the roads going south, anxious to try the beaches of New England, the Carolinas, Florida and even Mexico.

Yet we are always near water. Even in Quebec we gravitate toward the lakes and rivers of the province, and tend to focus much of our summer activity on fishing and water sports. Ski chalets are suddenly transformed into summer cottages and, after a rigorous game of tennis or eighteen holes of golf, we try to end the day with a cooling swim or an hour or two of wind-surfing. The roads are full once again, but the roof racks are now carrying wind-surf boards and small sail-boats instead of winter skis. There are the same people on the same routes, but they're now savouring the summer.

Summer is also a time for celebrating the great outdoors. We strip to the bare necessities and spend as much time outside with friends and family as we can, indulging in that great North American tradition, the barbecue, while sipping beer, tanning, and all the time defying winter to come back too soon.

As Québécois we need to be with others, to talk, to listen – and to tease. We've found the ideal formula to make this happen – the festival. This is a sort of gathering of the clans. We have hundreds of festivals during the summer celebrating everything from jazz, blueberries, humour and pigs, to camping, apples, folk music and theatre. Some of these festivals have achieved an international reputation. All are delightful, enabling the Québécois to satisfy their wish to eat, dance, talk and drink together. Before long, and usually too quickly for the sun-worshippers, there is a hint of cold in the air. Each day becomes a little shorter. The fireplaces and woodstoves have to be lit earlier in the evening, and weekends are spent stacking firewood closer to the back door. All the jobs which have been avoided so skillfully throughout the summer months must now be taken on. The rites of autumn begin: windows are caulked, those extra rolls of roof insulation are put into place, the eavestrough emptied of branches and leaves, and the hedges tied with protective snowfencing in anticipation of powerful storms. Winter is coming.

Yet autumn is also a time of exhilaration. Nobody has to organize a festival of colour in Quebec – that has already been done by nature. In September and October, the greens, yellows, oranges, reds and browns of the changing leaves dominate the whole province. Artists come to Quebec from around the world to paint, to be inspired, to thrill in disbelief as the forests seem to be lit by brilliantly-coloured spotlights. Once again the roads fill with traffic, but this time with "peepers". Among them are regular tourists who make their annual autumn trip to Quebec. Others come from abroad on organized "colour tours". Most of them are the Québécois and Québécoises who are drawn to the country roads each year in a sort of cleansing pilgrimage before the coming of the snow – a final look at the green-brown fields which will soon be covered until the spring.

For most Québécois winter is more than simply outdoor sports and vintage wines. Like the rest of the country, we have to work, study, raise our families, and create. In Quebec most of this happens in the city. I'm a Montrealer myself, "un Montréalais", and still have a special place in my heart for that great island city.

By any standard, Montreal is cosmopolitan. Almost half the population of the province lives there now, a whopping three million people, and fully one-third of those are from one of the many ethnic groups which combine to make Montreal such a stimulating place to live. The English, Scots, Italians, Greeks, Turks, Haitains and Vietnamese – to name but a few – have added to the cultural fabric of Quebec. They have contributed a great deal to our overall growth and, more importantly, to raising our level of maturity and awareness as a people. They have brought with them their ideas, their traditions – and their foods. Montreal has over 3,000 restaurants, many of them designed to introduce the uneducated palate to the addictive pleasures of "ethnic food". In fact there are entire streets in Montreal with nothing but restaurants, both ethnic and traditional, where customers are encouraged to come with their favourite wines from home. A real delight that makes for a very inexpensive evening.

I miss Montreal when I'm away for too long. I need my regular dose of "total immersion", a few days of bathing in a pleasant mixture of different languages and cultures. Where else can you celebrate St. John the Baptist Day (Quebec's patron saint), St. Andrew's Day and Canada Day with equal fervour, and with all the same people? Indeed, Montrealers especially look forward to St. Patrick's Day in March, when the beer sold in most of the brasseries is dyed green in honour of the Irish. Green beer and *tourtière* – why not?

Montreal is also the meeting place of the two great historic languages of North America, English and French. There are few other cities in the world where you can hear conversations in both these languages simultaneously! I always get a kick out of the number of people who switch constantly between English and French, and who feel just as comfortable in either. As a youngster, with an Anglophone mother and Francophone father, I never realized what that really meant. I had to leave Montreal to appreciate it. But I marvel today when, sitting on a bus or the Metro, I hear people switch several times within the same conversation, or follow an exchange in which each continues to speak in his or her own mother tongue. There is something totally unique about that, something "Montréalais".

But for all of Quebec, and much of northeastern North America, Montreal means serious shopping. There's the Rue St. Catherine, with its multi-storey department stores, its hundreds of boutiques catering to one of the most fashion-conscious people in the world, its constant flow of window-shoppers and strollers. And underneath the Rue Ste. Catherine are nine miles of underground shopping plazas, most of them now interconnected, containing over 1,000 stores and boutiques – Quebec's way of coping with the rigours of winter in a modern world.

Early last century Montreal became the centre of North America's fur trade. It remains so today, but the city has also evolved into the fashion centre of Canada, the place where you can buy that long-sought article, or have something made that has that special Quebec flair.

As Montrealers we are very likely to hide the fact that we have developed a coveted uniqueness in other areas as well. In theatre, for example, Montreal has become the home of a number of innovative companies which have to their credit a long list of prestigious international awards. The same is true of the fields of dance and music. Who can forget Charles Dutoit and l'Orchestre Symphonique de Montréal, easily Canada's finest orchestra. Montreal has grown into one of the most supportive cities on the continent, largely because of its culturally-conscious population, long accustomed to having the best. This has earned it the reputation of being Canada's cultural capital and, even better, it all happens in one of the safest cities in the world.

None of this could occur, however, were it not for the city's very dynamic business, industrial and financial sectors, which are growing at an unparalleled rate. It sort of makes you strut a little. In fact, most non-Montrealers will tell you frankly that Montrealers strut quite a lot. While I hate to admit it, I guess there is a grain of truth in what they say. We sometimes feel that we're the only real city in Quebec and that all the others are just big villages!

Those are fighting words in the province, especially in Quebec City. Indeed, there has been a rivalry between the two cities which dates all the way back to the seventeenth century. In addition to being founded some thirty-four years before Montreal, Quebec City remained considerably larger until the end of the last century, and was not above reminding Montreal of its relative status in various ways — some subtle, and others less so. During the early days of the colony, just as Montreal was beginning to establish itself, Quebec frequently used its strategic position on the St. Lawrence River to Montreal's disadvantage. All ships coming from France, for example — even those arranged by Montrealers — had to pass Quebec City before sailing on to Montreal. Arriving at the end of a rough sea voyage of many weeks, often in vessels not much larger than a small fishing boat, captains and their crew put in first at Quebec City where they found warm beds and local brew. Unfortunately, indignant Montrealers lost a number of precious cargoes over the years which were bought by the merchants of Quebec City, and sometimes resold for an additional profit in Montreal.

Even more sensitive was the case of women. A number of ships were sent out by the King of France with prospective wives for the predominantly male settlers in the colony. A boon to be sure! However, historians have recently come across correspondence in which Montrealers plead with the French authorities to send the next scheduled bridal ship to Montreal first. The most attractive women, they explained, were claimed first in Quebec City or Trois-Rivières. By the time the ships arrived in Montreal ...! Indeed, for many years Quebec City was reputed to have the most beautiful women in the province. And while the women are indeed very striking in Quebec City, anybody who has ever eaten lunch at an outdoor café in downtown Montreal on a summer day will surely attest to the equality which now exists in that area.

The rivalry is usually more humorous than aggressive. They are both wonderful cities and, as a Montréalais who has been based in Quebec City for about ten years, I can attest to all the joys of living there. Quebec City is a truly superb place, and I have grown to enjoy it immensely.

The only walled city north of Mexico, it is far more spectacular than Montreal, and has a dignified charm about it that is quite unique. It has its own vigorous blend of restaurants, theatres and architecture which combine to make living in the province's capital an entirely seductive experience.

Most of all, though, Quebec City is the people. Perhaps this is because of the different traditions here, or because the population numbers only 500,000 — I'm still not sure why. I do know, however, that in general the people in Quebec City are a little more graceful, and the pace of life is just a bit slower than in Montreal. There is a unique sense of quiet dignity about the place. Montrealers are definitely more earthy, and their sense of humour a shade more bizarre by comparison.

These are rather daring sentiments for a Montreal native to admit publicly, especially one who lives in Quebec City, but who claims the need to return to Montreal for a regular booster. Had I been gone too long? Was I in need of a cultural transfusion? Was there something in the drinking water in Quebec City? It would have to be tested scientifically. I am an inveterate jogger, and I have a wide range of running shirts, including those of the arch rival Montréal Canadiens and Quebec Nordiques hockey teams. One day, when in Montreal for a business trip, I decided to throw fate to the wind and jog through the downtown streets wearing my Nordiques sweater. Drivers stopped their cars to yell. Truckers blared their horns. Women swore at me from store fronts, and a group of young teenage boys and girls made a number of totally unwholesome suggestions. A shattering experience, to be sure!

In order to be scientifically sound, I realized to my chagrin that I would have to proceed with the same experiment in reverse. I would have to wear my Canadiens sweater on a similar run through Quebec City's downtown area. Would Phase II progress to physical abuse? But true to form, the Quebec City drivers and passers-by merely shook their heads in horrified disgust. Much to my embarrassment the only vocal reaction was from a group of visiting Montreal businessmen who lowered their car windows and proceeded to clap and yell, unashamedly encouraging the locals to join in. My point had been made. And to my great surprise, I realized then that some of Quebec City had rubbed off on me.

But there is much more to Quebec than its two biggest cities. Having lived all over the province, I never cease to be amazed at the uniqueness which characterizes each of the various regions. We lived for a year about 1,000 miles northeast of Montreal in a place called Schefferville – no roads for 400 miles – and loved the stark and rugged beauty, the total silence that cannot be found in the cities. We have also lived in the Laurentians – who could possibly dislike living in a postcard that changes every few days? – while, after four years in the Eastern Townships, I feel certain that we are destined to retire there.

I've also had the opportunity to travel extensively throughout Quebec and have been able to discover something new and typically Québécois each time. I remember the fjord-like terrain of the Charlevoix, the spectacular sights of the Gaspe, the Beauce region with that special local accent that makes you want to come back soon, and the Saguenay-Lac St. Jean area which is almost a world unto itself – the scenery designed for a film set, the people exuding that special charm. They are known by the Québécois as the "baluets", the blueberry people, because of the way they used to pronounce the word "bluet". The berry is found up there in abundance, and used by the locals to make a delicious drink that can knock your socks off!

I guess I have a kind of love affair with this province of mine, and I still haven't seen it all. Before too long, I want to uncover the secrets of the upper reaches of Quebec's North Shore, where one can still get a sense of what it was like in those first days of the colony. I also want to go back to the James Bay region, where the province is completing a series of hydroelectric dams that will ensure both our economic survival and a non-nuclear environment for decades to come. In fact, when the project is finally completed, the total water and land area in the region falling under the jurisdiction of Hydro-Quebec will be equivalent to the size of England! Quite impressive – and all built by the Québécois. That's not a bad achievement for six-and-a-half million people, is it?

The James Bay project has become a symbol for most Québécois; a concrete sign that we will make it into the twenty-first century. Twenty-five years ago we set ourselves a major challenge, one taken up by few other peoples throughout history. Here we were, six million souls or so, living on a continent surrounded by 275 million English-speaking people. For two centuries we had held on proudly and tenaciously to our language, culture and heritage. Indeed, the province's motto, "Je me souviens" ("I remember"), sums up very well that complex process which requires that we remember our past when planning the future.

However, by the late 1950s, we realized that if we really wanted our culture to survive we had to become a functional part of the twentieth century. We had to show the world that we no longer wished to live a marginal nineteenth-century existence. We had to become a determining element of Quebec's economy, we had to modernize the province, and we had to train our children for this new society in a totally revitalized school system. The Quiet Revolution of the 1960s had begun! In a dizzying process that captured the hearts and minds of the entire population, we gave ourselves the tools to catch up with the rest of the world, and transformed our entire society in just a few short years.

We also set ourselves new goals. We wanted to maintain our distinct cultural existence, to live in French, and still be an integral part of Canada and of North America. We rejected the idea of permanently living a museum existence, wearing our "ceintures flèchees", playing our fiddles and dancing our jigs. Well, on weekends maybe, but on weekdays we had to develop our aeronautics industry, our transportation sector, our space technology, our research facilities, our Stock Exchange – our James Bay projects.

I lived this period. This was Quebec's 1960s experience. Every nation lived that decade in its own unique way – we rebuilt our society. It's difficult to capture on paper the profound depth of those changes. Even our language changed. The French we use now is definitely not the archaic anglicized French that I learned as a child just after World War II. We were told by the fathers and mothers of the new Quebec that, if we really wished to live in the twentieth century, our language would have to evolve also. So we proceeded to learn a new language, a little awkwardly and self-consciously at first, but learn it we did. It was all part of the most exciting time of my life.

The French we speak today is still distinctly Québécois, and reflects both the world and the lifestyle we've chosen for ourselves. Some of our words are different from those spoken in France – mainly those we have borrowed from the Amerindians and the English, or the vocabulary we have had to invent ourselves, such as for baseball. However, we usually understand our French cousins perfectly well, just as we converse easily with our partners in the forty other Francophone nations of the world. It is more a question of accent and rhythm than of vocabulary, and can be compared to the differences that exist between North American English and that which is spoken in England, Scotland or Australia. Like everything else, we even speak with a special Québécois flavour.

As Québécois and Québécoises, we have everything going for us. We have one of the most beautiful places on earth in which to live, and we own resources that are the envy of the world. Most importantly, though, we have been able to prove to both ourselves and to the world that we have the total commitment that it takes to ensure that we will not merely survive as a people, but grow. The Québécois are quite lucky really – we've been able to live a dream.

The Gatineau Hills (this and previous page), part of the ancient Canadian Shield, are set in the timbered wilderness of Gatineau Park. The Gatineau River courses across the park and the surrounds of Chelsea, running on through the district of La Pêche (above), or Wakefield. The lumber floating in its waters follows a traditional logging route down to the Ottawa River.

The Laurentians (facing page and overleaf), part of the Precambrian Canadian Shield covering most of the province, are laced with waterways, rivers and lakes, such as inky-blue Lac Tremblant (facing page top) and Lac Rond (facing page bottom) at Sainte-Adèle, which provide endless facilities for water-sport enthusiasts. The Sainte-Adèle writers' and artists' colony is a tribute to the area's great natural beauty, and its theater contributes to the famed night-life of the Laurentians.

From the 967-metre-high summit (left) of Mont Tremblant (these pages) one gazes down at the Laurentians from their highest point, over a wonderland where the low winter sun twinkles on the ice and enthusiastic skiers dot the slopes around Gray Rocks Resort (top).

Winter sports take over Lac Tremblant (above) with the ice, and
Mont Tremblant Ski Resort (these pages) is a blur of colourful
skiers taking advantage of one of North America's best-equipped
resorts. Québec receives an average of 130 inches of snow on its
slopes each year between October and April, making the
province a skiers' paradise.

Above: Montreal (these pages and overleaf) seen from Mount Royal Park, site of the Mount Royal Cemetery (top). Facing page bottom: the 8,670-foot-long, cantilever Jacques Cartier Bridge strung across the St. Lawrence River. Molson Brewery (facing page top), founded in 1786, is Canada's oldest continuously operating brewery.

Against the plate glass of Montreal's business quarter flutter the flags (facing page) of Québec and Canada. Above: the balcony of the Hôtel de Ville, from which de Gaulle made his famous "*Vive le Québec libre*" speech. Neighbouring Nelson Column, honouring the famous British Admiral, was built in 1809, and so predates London's similar monument by thirty-four years. Strangely, it faces neither into the square, nor towards the river.

The Olympic Stadium (above), a giant concrete mollusc, was
finally completed eleven years after the 1976 games at huge cost,
is also known as the "Big O", or the "Big Owe". In winter, its
infield becomes a skating rink (facing page bottom). Marathons
(facing page top) make an extended running track of Montreal's
streets. Entertainments offered on St. Helen's Island include the
grounds of World Fair Expo 67, for which the fan-like French
and tiered British pavillions (overleaf) were built. They are now
part of the annual exhibition, "Man and His World".

Paul de Chomedey, Sieur de Maisonneuve, commemorated by a
statue (facing page) in the Place d'Armes, was sent from France
on a sacred mission to build a Christian city in a pagan land.
He founded Montreal. Notre-Dame church (above and facing
page), and St. Joseph's Oratory (overleaf) vindicate his faith.
Indeed, Brother André, who caused the Oratory to be built,
defied the depression years by placing a statue of St. Joseph in
the then roofless church, saying "If he wants a roof over his
head he'll get it."

Montreal is a vibrant city, thriving at the foot of its extinct volcano, Mount Royal. The street markets (these pages) display tiers of vividly coloured vegetables and intricate knick-knacks. Overleaf: the view over McGill University across the city towards the Upper Harbour of the St. Lawrence River. The harbour is glimpsed behind I.M. Pei's remarkable Place Ville Marie, an extensive shopping centre dominated by the forty-five-storey, cruciform Royal Bank Tower.

ARRÊT STOP

Savourez Coca-Cola

RESTAURANT CHEZ JEAN-PAUL
VIANDE FUMÉE · SHISH-KEBAB · SOUVLAKI · SALADE GRECQUE
HAMBURGERS · SOUS-MARIN · METS ITALIENS

Le SOUVLAKI et SALADE GRECQUE

RUE STE-CATHE...

basilaire 2

basilaire 1

VISA Desjardins

promenade

Montrealers are apparently so proud of their city that the walls of St. Catherine Street (facing page top) are painted with its image, and outdoor cafés, such as Café Rue Sherbrooke (top), seem designed to allow people to gaze at leisure on attractions like the ivory-coloured iron trelliswork of balconies (above) in the Papineau Quarter. Of course, when the city is frosted with snow (overleaf), the centrally-heated enticements of the Complèxe Desjardins (facing page bottom) might prevail.

The area of Québec's Eastern Townships (these pages and overleaf), inhabited by immigrant New Englanders, was further populated by Loyalists in flight after the American War of Independence. The name Eastern Townships arose to distinguish these towns from those west of Montreal, which are now in Ontario. The region is also known, understandably, as the "Garden of Québec" and is famous for its dairy and livestock farms, such as those in the Iron Hill area (these pages) flanking the Iron Hill Road (above and facing page bottom). Overleaf: autumn trees form an arch of ochre and copper at Saxby Corner.

La Mauricie National Park (these pages) was created in 1970, and incorporates Québec's Laurentian Highlands, which are riddled with lakes and rivers. Lac en Croix Brook (facing page) presents an unfettered wildness, whereas Lac Edouard (above) shows the tamer face of La Mauricie where boats or windsurfboards can be safely accommodated.

Canoeing (right) and many other watersports draw enthusiasts from all over Canada to La Mauricie National Park (these pages). However, for those who prefer not to surf or sail or get into the water in any way, La Mauricie's lakeland beauty offers great visual relaxation. Its 154 lakes, such as Lac à la Pêche (below), and innumerable waterways (facing page) are a refreshing sight for tired city eyes.

Appropriately, Québec province's motto is *Je me souviens*, "I remember", and the air of turreted, French-Renaissance grandeur in the walled city of Quebec, the earliest stronghold of French culture in North America, gives it a wistful poise. The copper-roofed Château Frontenac (below and facing page bottom), and the Parliament Buildings (facing page top) standing across from the Champlain monument to Quebec's founder, recall the words of Rupert Brooke, "Is there any city in the world that stands so nobly as Quebec?".

Overleaf: the 1892 Château Frontenac on its promontory over the St. Lawrence, seen from the Champlain Boulevard. The Château is a palatial hotel built on the original site of Samuel de Champlain's Fort St. Louis, which was his residence as governor. It looks out over the wall, and over the cliffs on which Quebec's Upper Town rests. These were scaled in a daring action by the British, under General Wolfe, in 1759. Both Wolfe and the renowned French general, Montcalm, died in the ensuing battle.

Old Quebec (these pages and overleaf) has withstood many a
seige, but those of "General January", as Nicholas I of Russia
called winter, and the onslaught of modern industry are harder
to resist. Nonetheless, the signs of an old fortress town are
everywhere. Throughout the eighteenth century the French and
British were almost continuously at war, and Quebec was in
daily danger of attack. Residual fortifications, and the sheer wall
girdling the Upper Town are Quebec's visible heritage from a
stormy past.

"The impression made upon the visitor by this Gibraltar of North America: its giddy heights; its citadel suspended, as it were, in the air, its picturesque streets and frowning gateways; and the splendid views which burst upon the eye at every turn: is at once unique and everlasting" – words as true of Quebec (these pages) today as when spoken by Charles Dickens in 1842. When viewed from certain vantage points, the city could almost still be set in 1842.

Instead of being bowed down under the weight of a Québec
winter, in February the Québécois erupt into life during the ten-
day Quebec Winter Carnival (these pages). The city's population
is doubled by visitors during these pre-Lent festivities, which
centre around the ice palace (facing page bottom). Its
illuminated, fairy-story style does not seem at all out of place
amid the intricate architecture of Quebec (overleaf) or, indeed,
among the astonishing ice sculptures surrounding it.

La Reine du Carnaval

QUÉBEC-ALBERTA

QUÉBEC-ALBERTA

QUÉBEC-AL

À LA DÉCOUVERTE DE L'AL

Quebec city (these pages and overleaf) is an explorers' paradise. Its vibrant colours and narrow streets beckon to one from the past and draw visitors further into their elegant world with every turn. It has been described as a city made for leisurely walking, and its continental terrace cafés and numerous restaurants assure the wanderer of frequent refreshment. French-style baking and European café life are all part of the charm of Quebec, a city which still cherishes the aspect and atmosphere of old France.

Streets lined with artists' work (top) are perhaps one of Quebec's legacies from France. Above: in St. Louis Street the smile of Bonhomme Carnaval presides over the famous Quebec Winter Carnival. Facing page: Rue Petit Champlain hung with decorative shop signs, lined with wrought-iron balconies and lit by lanterns overhanging the street. Potted Christmas trees by doorways give the city streets a strong neighbourhood atmosphere.

The St. Lawrence River, spanned by Quebec's two famous bridges (facing page bottom), the Quebec Bridge and Pierre Laporte Bridge, affords the city much in the way of water sport facilities and marinas (this page). However, Quebec caters for most tastes in leisure activities, including golf (facing page top).

The topography of Québec helps to make skiing extremely popular as many first-rate ski sites are very close to Quebec city. Mont Ste-Anne is only a day's excursion by car from there, and its summit (facing page), 875 metres high, is ideal for downhill skiing.

Just before its confluence with the St. Lawrence, the Montmorency River drops over eighty-three metres at Montmorency Falls, making these falls actually higher than Niagara's. In winter its spray freezes to form a remarkable "sugarloaf" block of ice and snow (above), providing tobogganers with a perfect slope.

These pages: Charlevoix County on the north shore of the St. Lawrence. Les Éboulements (above) are named for landslides occurring after the 1663 earthquake, which was so severe that a mountain on the bank became an island in the St. Lawrence River. The setting of Baie-Sainte-Paul, between two promontories at the mouth of the Gouffre River, makes the landscape around it (facing page bottom) very popular with artists. Facing page top: St-Joseph-de-la-Rive.

On the south side of the St. Lawrence River, not far from the border with New Brunswick, lie the scenic towns of St-Eusèbe (facing page bottom), where pale roads bisect gently undulating hills and expanses of parti-coloured forest, Notre-Dame-du-Lac (above) and the land around Dégelis (facing page top). Overleaf: the area of St-Octave-de-Métis.

The lighthouse at Pointe-des-Monts (facing page) overlooks the rugged northeast coast of the Gaspé Peninsula from the south bank of the St. Lawrence River. The Gaspé Peninsula, named from the Micmac Indian word *gaspeg*, meaning "the end of the earth", lies where the St. Lowrence flows through the Détroit d'Honguedo into the Gulf of St. Lawrence. Above: landscape south of the St. Lawrence River.

The sheer, limestone cliffs of Cap Gaspé (below) in Forillon National Park (these pages) have been formed by constant tidal action. The mysterious presence of hardy alpine flora on these cliffs has not yet been explained by botanists. Facing page: a waterfall along the La Chute trail.

Forillon National Park (these pages) on the Gaspé Peninsula is renowned for its forested beauty, burnished and reddened by autumn.

Saint-Joachim-de-Tourelle (facing page bottom) on the Gaspé
Peninsula (facing page top and overleaf), a fishing and
agricultural community since 1916, was almost destroyed by a
landslide in 1963. Above: the cliffs of Mont Joli. The rose-gold
limestone of Percé Rock (last pages), the culmination of the
Peninsula's beauty, stands off Mont Joli at the end of a
sandbank. Centuries ago the rock had three arches, then two.
Today only one remains; one of the former arches became a
separate block known as the Obelisk.